First World War
and Army of Occupation
War Diary
France, Belgium and Germany

2 DIVISION
2 Light Brigade
London Regiment
6th (City of London) Battalion (Rifles)
1 March 1919 - 23 October 1919

WO95/1374/6

The Naval & Military Press Ltd
www.nmarchive.com
Published in association with The National Archives

Published by

The Naval & Military Press Ltd

Unit 10 Ridgewood Industrial Park,

Uckfield, East Sussex,

TN22 5QE England

Tel: +44 (0) 1825 749494

www.naval-military-press.com

www.nmarchive.com

This diary has been reprinted in facsimile from the original. Any imperfections are inevitably reproduced and the quality may fall short of modern type and cartographic standards.

© Crown Copyright
Images reproduced by permission of The National Archives, London, England, 2015.

Contents

Document type	Place/Title	Date From	Date To
Heading	WO95/1374/6		
Heading	2 Division 2 Light Brigade 6 London Regt 1919 Mar 1919 Oct From 58 Div 174 Bde		
War Diary	Nievenheim	01/03/1919	15/03/1919
War Diary	Zons-Am-Rhein	16/03/1919	22/03/1919
War Diary	Zons	23/03/1919	31/03/1919
War Diary	Zons-Am-Rhein	01/04/1919	06/04/1919
War Diary	Nettesheim	07/04/1919	31/05/1919
Miscellaneous	Headquarters, 2nd Light Brigade.	30/06/1919	30/06/1919
War Diary	Nettesheim	01/06/1919	17/06/1919
War Diary	Ehrenfeld	18/06/1919	30/06/1919
Miscellaneous	Headquarters 2nd Light Brigade	31/07/1919	31/07/1919
War Diary	Ehrenfeld	01/07/1919	01/07/1919
War Diary	Nettesheim	02/07/1919	09/07/1919
War Diary	Ohligs	10/07/1919	23/10/1919

WO 05/1374| 6

2 (~~LIGHT~~) DIVISION

2 LIGHT BRIGADE

6 LONDON REGT

1919 MAR — 1919 OCT

FROM 58 DIV MYBDF

WAR DIARY or INTELLIGENCE SUMMARY

Army Form C. 2118.

6 London Rifles Vol 27

Place	Date	Hour	Summary of Events and Information	Remarks and references to Appendices
	March 1919			
	1.		Everyone for Germany in vain. JM	
NIEDERHEIM	2.		Arrived DELRATH station near COLOGNE at 0130 hrs (approx) and detrained. JM Billeted in DELRATH (A,B Coys, Drm Hrs & Tpt), NIEDERHEIM (HQ Coy) and UKERATH (D Coy) — JM	
			Met in 5th Infantry Bde (HQ DORMAGEN), 2nd Division (HQ DÜREN) JM	
			VI Corps and 2nd Army (HQ COLOGNE) JM	
	3		General cleaning & cleaning up JM	
	4		do do JM	
	5		do do Lieut (A/Major) F.G. TOLWORTHY MC to leave JM	
	6		Inspection by B.G.C. 5th Bde JM Lieut (A/Capt) J.H.W. IDRIS MC	
	7		General training JM Lieut HM HODGES to leave. JM B Coy relieved 52nd Light Infantry on Munition Factory Guard, DORMAGEN JM	
	8		General training JM Lieut W.H. BRASHER to leave JM	
	9		Church Parade JM	
	10		General Training JM D Coy moved to STÜRZELBERG JM	
	11		Companies match practice morning & Reference Learning by	

WAR DIARY
INTELLIGENCE SUMMARY

Army Form C. 2118.

Page 2

Place	Date	Hour	Summary of Events and Information	Remarks and references to Appendices
	11 (cont)		52nd Light Infantry at ZONS-AM-RHEIN. Draft of 174 O.R. from 10th KRRC joined. Also Lieut. (A/Capt) F. HALL, Lieut. H.T. FICE, 2/Lt. T.C. WELSH, 2/Lt. A.N. SCHAEFFER, 2/Lt. P.J. EGGAR.	
	12		Funeral Party for funeral of O.R. died in Cologne.	
			General training.	
	13		do.	
	14		do.	
			D Coy relieved B Coy on DORMAGEN Factory Guard.	
			B Coy take on STURZELBURG Billets.	
			2/Lt (A/Capt) C.E. MEE reported.	
			R.H.O'D. MAULE-FFINCH reported from leave.	
			Name of Burgen changed to "Schloss Durcken".	
	15		do.	
ZONS-AM-RHEIN	16		HQ, A & C Coys & Oun Hors moved by march route to ZONS-AM-RHEIN arriving about 1230h. Transport moved to RHEINFELD. B Coy remained at RHEINFELD. B Coy remained at STURZELBURG. Billets in ZONS 9 RHEINFELD taken on from 52nd K.L. and 52nd R.F. took on Billets vacated in NIEVENHEIM and DELRATH. Battalion takes on responsibility for the defence of the STURZELBURG-BENRATH ferry.	

WAR DIARY
or
INTELLIGENCE SUMMARY

(Erase heading not required.)

Army Form C. 2118.

Page 3

Place	Date	Hour	Summary of Events and Information	Remarks and references to Appendices
ZONS-AM-RHEIN	17		General Training. 2/Lt. A.M.H. Buel & 2/Lt. E.A. Bowers-Taylor from Reinf. A/Capt. S.R. Scott joined.	
	18		do & baths. Capt. H.B. Owden joined. 2/Lt. L.C. Leapman M.C. & 2/Lt. C.A. Fuller joined from Leave. A/Capt. Cemee proceeded to Dismd. Camp, Dieren to Italy. 2/Lt. Atheridge to Leave. 2/Lt. T.C. Welsh, 2/Lt. H.G. Ecce Lt. C.R. Crossland M.C., 2/Lt. T.C. Welsh, 2/Lt. H.G. Ecce Lt. V. Cancellor to 2/17 Bn. London Regt.	
	19		General Training. 2/Lt. P. Astles to 2/17 4th London Regt.	
	20		do.	
	21		do. C Coy relieved D Coy on Dormagen Factory Gd. B Coy moved to Zons. D Coy mvd to Storzelsorg. 2/Lt. Jno. Matcham to Leave.	
	22		do. Lt.(A/Capt.) A.M. Laird M.C., Lt.(A/Capt.) K.M. Blofeld M.C., 2/Lt. E.D. Kimber, 2/Lt. G.E. Cripps, H.V. McGowan, Lt. W.T. James, 2/Lt. E.G. Willmott, Lt. G.E. Scott joined.	

WAR DIARY
or
INTELLIGENCE SUMMARY.
(Erase heading not required.)

Army Form C. 2118.

Page 4

Place	Date	Hour	Summary of Events and Information	Remarks and references to Appendices
ZONS	23		Church Parade	
	24		Test manning of STURZELBURG-BENRATH ferry defences	
	25		General training. Lt. Col. C.S. Benson D.S.O. proceeded to England on duty and Major Gap Farrell D.S.O. assumed Command of Battalion.	
	26		do	
	27		do	
	28		Practice manning of the Rhine Ferry (STURZELBURG-BENRATH)	
	29		General training. Lt. H.M. HODGES from leave. Capt. F. Hall to England on duty	
	30		Church Parade. 2/Lt. H.F. WILLCOCKS to leave	
	31		General training. Capt. H.B. OWDEN to leave	

Capt. & Adjutant.
for Major Comdg. G. Howitzer Regt.

WAR DIARY
or
INTELLIGENCE SUMMARY.
(Erase heading not required.)

Army Form C. 2118.

April 1919

Place	Date	Hour	Summary of Events and Information	Remarks and references to Appendices
ZONS-AM-RHEIN	1		Strength of Bn. 49 Off. 982 OR. Number present 31 Off. 615 OR. General Training	
	2		do. Capt. & QuarterMaster F.G. LOVETT to leave.	
	3		do. and Baths. Lieut. W.T. JAMES to D.A.M., 2nd Army. A Company and part of B. proceed to Artillery Barracks, Cologne, for duty with 12th Lancers. T/Capt. C.H.L. DUBB to leave.	
	4		do.	
	5		do. By Coy. Preparations for move. Advance party leave. 2/Capt. T.J. MUMFORD M.C. to leave 2/Lieut. O.E. CAPPS to leave Capt. W.D. COLERIDGE demobilize	
	6		Battalion moved into the villages of NETTESHEIM & BUTZHEIM & FRIXHEIM (H.Q., C Coy. Tpt. & Dml. Stores, billets reserved for A Coy.), ANSTEL (B Coy.) and ECKUM (D Coy.) Transferred to 99th Bde. renamed. Arrived 1530 hrs. 2nd Light Bde.	
NETTESHEIM	7		General Training and organization	
	8		do. Lieut. A.H. ETHERIDGE from leave. T/Lieut. M.T. ALLEN reported for duty	

WAR DIARY
or
INTELLIGENCE SUMMARY.

(Erase heading not required.)

Army Form C. 2118.

Place	Date	Hour	Summary of Events and Information	Remarks and references to Appendices
NETTESHEIM	9		General Training starts.	
	10		General Training. Lt. Col. J.B. BRADY, D.S.O. joined and resumed command of Battalion. 2/Lieut. R.O. EVANS joined for duty.	
	11		do. A/Capt. J.C.L. GIRDLESTONE & T/Lieut. J. CROMIE joined for duty & proceeded to 1st. Regt TM Bty. Lieut. L.C. WATSON from leave.	
	12		do. Lieut. H.M. HODGES demobilized. 2/Lt. P.I. EGGAR to Convoc. 2/Lt. W.J. BROWN from leave.	
	13		Church Parade. 2/Lt R.B. PATTINSON from leave.	
	14		General Training. 2/Lt E. MORRIS from leave.	
	15		do. 2/Lt. R.J. LEACH joined for duty. Capt. A.M. LAIRD to leave.	
	16		Battalion Route March. Capt. the Rev. G.H. BARNICOAT C.F. joined for duty.	
	17		General Training & Baths. 2/Major F.G. TOLLWORTHY M.C. demobilized. 2/Major J.H.W. IDRIS, M.C. demobilized. Lieut. W.H. BRASHER to Bde. as Asst. Staff Capt. 2/Lieut. J.N.L. MATCHAM from leave.	

WAR DIARY
or
INTELLIGENCE SUMMARY.

(Erase heading not required.)

Army Form C. 2118.

Instructions regarding War Diaries and Intelligence Summaries are contained in F. S. Regs., Part II. and the Staff Manual respectively. Title pages will be prepared in manuscript.

Place	Date	Hour	Summary of Events and Information	Remarks and references to Appendices
	18		Good Friday. JM Voluntary Church service & Sports. JM Lieut G.L. Scott from leave. JM	
	19		General Training "Balkan" JM 2/Capt. J.J. Ball Jones for duty & assumed command of D Coy. JM 2/Lt. B. Lamberth joined for duty JM 2/Lt. L.C. Leapman (Armourer) JM Lieut. L.G. Watson (Armourer) JM 2/Lieut. D. Frost joined for duty JM + J. Trim joined for duty JM	
	20		Church Parades. JM Capt. H.B. Owden from leave	
	21		Easter Monday JM Voluntary Church service and sport. JM 2/Lt. H.T. Willcocks from leave.	
	22		Battalion Route March JM 2/Lt. F.G. Willmott to Bde. HQ. to assist Civil Staff Capt. JM	
	23		General Training JM Brigadier General Comg. 2d Light Bde. inspects Bn. JM whole training, including billets and dinners. JM 2/Capt. T.J. Munford MC from leave. JM Lieut. J.M. C. Gowan to Etherton Camp at Newmarket 7/JM Major J.A.I. Farrell DSO. to leave (1 month) JM	

1577 Wt. W10791/1773 500,000 1/15 D. D. & L. A.D.S.S./Forms/C. 2118.

Army Form C. 2118.

WAR DIARY
or
INTELLIGENCE SUMMARY.
(Erase heading not required.)

Instructions regarding War Diaries and Intelligence Summaries are contained in F. S. Regs., Part II. and the Staff Manual respectively. Title pages will be prepared in manuscript.

Place	Date	Hour	Summary of Events and Information	Remarks and references to Appendices
	24		General Training & Baths. Education Classes JMM	
	25		General Training & Education Classes JMM 2/Lieut. J.N.L. MATCHAM (temporily) JMM 2/Lieut. R.B. COOKE M.C. to Oxford JMM Education Course. JMM	
	26		General Training JMM rehearsal of parade for inspection by Major-General Commanding 39th Division. JMM 2/Lieut. F.J. DERMENT joined for duty JMM & Capt. E.H.L. BUBB & Capt. Adm. F.G. LOVETT from leave JMM	
	27		Church Parade JMM	
	28		General Training Education Classes JMM	
	29		Baths & General Training & Education Classes. JMM	

WAR DIARY
or
INTELLIGENCE SUMMARY.

(Erase heading not required.)

Army Form C. 2118.

Place	Date	Hour	Summary of Events and Information	Remarks and references to Appendices
F	30		Inspection of Battalion by Major General Commanding Brigade Division. JWM. Leis. J.H. PARTRIDGE to Command JWM. 51 Off 918 O.R. JWM 30 Off 565 O.R. JWM Strength P.B. No Prisoners.	

J.W. Newton
Capt. & Adjt.
6th London Regt.

WAR DIARY
or
INTELLIGENCE SUMMARY

6th Bn London Reg
May 1919

Army Form C. 2118.

Place	Date	Hour	Summary of Events and Information	Remarks and references to Appendices
NETTESHEIM	1		General Training & Education	
	2		Battalion Route march. 2/Capt W.Ball to have lecture by Commands Reinnts Brome Rev on the "many during the war". Bdr Gno officer and Officers NCOs	
	3		General Training & Education. 1 Offr +62 OR return from detached duty with Cavalry Div. Cologne	
	4		Church Parade	
	5		Inspection of Battalion by Brig. Gen. MILDREN	
	6		General Training, Education. 4/Batho Major E.PEATFIELD MC reports	
	7		General Training & Education	
	8		Battalion Route march	
	9		General Training & Education Plank march for athl. 6	
	10		General Training. 2/Capt A.M. LAIRD M.C. from leave. 2/Lt KHOO MOULE-EFINCH to Corns " A.W. SCHAEFFER to Permanant C.J Engury Divn. Inspection of billets by Brig Gen. R.A.M. CURRIE, CMG, DSO Comdg. 2nd Lt Bde	

WAR DIARY
or
INTELLIGENCE SUMMARY.
(Erase heading not required.)

Army Form C. 2118.

Place	Date	Hour	Summary of Events and Information	Remarks and references to Appendices
	11		Church Parade	
	12		General Training & Education	
	13		— do. — 2/Lt P.J.EGGAR from Cmnd. Bn. Dark Room (Photographic) established. Lieut. AWKADIAN Jones for duty as Education Officer. Lecture by Bishop of Lichfield on "The Earlier Democracy (Athens)"	
	14		Inspection of Battalion by Lt. Col. J.B.BRAN, DSO (Commanding Officer) Lecture by Rev. Rev. M.KNIGHT on "The State & the Drink Traffic".	
	15		Inspection of Battalion by Brig.Genl. R.A.M. CURRIE, CMG, DSO, Commanding 2nd Light Brigade. 2/Lt H.GANDER to leave	
	16		General Training - preparation for inspection by C in C. 2/Lt. W.V. BROWN to special leave to Brussels	
	17		Inspection of Battalion by General Sir William ROBERTSON, GCB, GCVO, DSO, ADC. Commanding in Chief British Army of the Rhine.	

WAR DIARY
or
INTELLIGENCE SUMMARY.
(Erase heading not required.)

Army Form C. 2118.

Place	Date	Hour	Summary of Events and Information	Remarks and references to Appendices
	18		Church Parade JM	
	19		General Training & Education JM	
	20		General Training, Baths & Education JM 2/Capt N Bain from leave JM 2/Lieut C.A. CRIPPS to Cripps Course (Edn.) JM 2/Lieut V TRIM to 58th Divn HQ JM Lecture by 2/Lt V. McCabe on "Wonderful Seeing" How it was made – JM	
	21		Route March (2+3 Coys) JM General Training (4+10 Coys) & Education JM Lecture by Mr Dixon Scott on "Imperial Routes – Land, Sea & Air" JM	
	22		Route March (1+4 Coys) JM General Training (2+3 Coys) & Education JM	
	23		General Training & Education JM do JM	Major J.S. FARRELL DSO from leave JM 2/Lt R.J. EGGAR to leave JM 2/Lt W.J. BROWN from Brussels leave JM
	24			
	25		Church Parade JM	
	26		General Training & Baths & Education JM	Major B. PLEATFIELD M.C. assumes command of B Coy. JM
	27		General Training, Education & Baths JM	

WAR DIARY
or
INTELLIGENCE SUMMARY.

(Erase heading not required.)

Army Form C. 2118.

Place	Date	Hour	Summary of Events and Information	Remarks and references to Appendices
	28		Battalion Route March. JWM	
	29		General Training & Education JWM	
	30		General Training JWM	
	31		General Training JWM	
			Lecture by Mr Walden Hair on "Poland Past & Present" JWM	
			Strength of Battalion 50 off. 918 O.R. JWM	
			On Command 32 off. 624 O.R. JWM	
			[signature]	
			[signature] Capt. & adjt.	
			6 Bn Rifle Brigade Rifles	

Headquarters,
2nd Light Brigade.
....

Herewith 'War Diary' for this Battalion, compiled for the month of June.

..................Lt. Colonel.
Commanding 6th Bn. London Regt.,

30th June 1919.

WAR DIARY
or
INTELLIGENCE SUMMARY.

(Erase heading not required.)

Army Form C. 2118.

6th Bn. London Regt.
June 1919.

Place	Date	Hour	Summary of Events and Information	Remarks and references to Appendices
Tottenham	1		Church Parade. Brig-Gen. Raym. Currie Cmg DSO attended	CAL
	2		General training & Education	CAL
	3		Battalion parade. Royal Salute for King's birthday. Sports during afternoon.	2/Lt B. Jester from leave. Battalion Guard Party. Lt-Col. J.B. Brady DSO attended	CAL
	4		Rifle Range	2/Lt J. McEwan from Elles; Course in England. Lt J.H. Partridge to leave. 2 O.R.s to course at Newmarket.	CAL
	5		General training & Education	8 O.R. at demob.	CAL
	6		General training & Education	2/Lt C.D. Linden to leave	CAL
	7		General training & Education		CAL
	8		Church Parade	Lt-Col. J.B. Brady from leave	CAL
	9		Holiday. Sports in afternoon	Capt. Rev. Perpetual Walton to demob for 1 month	CAL
	10		General training & Education		CAL

WAR DIARY
or
INTELLIGENCE SUMMARY.
(Erase heading not required.)

Army Form C. 2118.

Place	Date	Hour	Summary of Events and Information	Remarks and references to Appendices
Vlamertinghe	11		Baths & General Training & Education	CW
	12		Baths & General Training & Education	CW
	13		General Training. Ammunition Guard at Pommern & Kruit Station relieved by 12th R.I.R.	CW
			(a/Capt T.L. Mumford Ret. to 2nd Lt. Ptte L. Staff Captain. 2/Lt. C.R. Fuller assumed duties of Capt.	CW
	14		General Training & Education	CW
			Major J.J. Farrell to B.H.Q. Capt. Lyn. Bird M.C. Lt. J.L. Scott	CW
	15		Church Parade	CW
			2/Lt. B. Jone to duty with 12th Lancers. Capt. S.R. Scott to duty with 12th Lancers. A PM	CW
	16		General Training & Education.	CW
			Capt. L.J. Batow M.C. to same Capt. B.N. Armstrong MC posted for duty as M.O. 2/Lt. as G. Lee joins for duty	CW
	17		General Training & Education.	CW
			2/Lt. P.J. Eger. to same Capt. Rev. Ingle joins for duty	CW
			Battalion left Vlamertinghi area. B & C Coys & Ho & 36 of A Coy direct to Poperinghe by Bus Rd. Bn. HQ. D Coy remainder of A Coy to Poelderine by march route	CW

Army Form C. 2118.

WAR DIARY
or
INTELLIGENCE SUMMARY.
(Erase heading not required.)

Instructions regarding War Diaries and Intelligence Summaries are contained in F. S. Regs., Part II. and the Staff Manual respectively. Title pages will be prepared in manuscript.

Place	Date	Hour	Summary of Events and Information	Remarks and references to Appendices
Ebenfels	18		Bn. HQ Stay remainder of A Coy. to Ebenfels beyond gate.	CW
	19.		Battalion supplying guards relieving by in emergency position. 2/Lt. R.B. Cartlesne from four course in Egypt.	CW
	20.		do do Major J.G. Parnell DSO to Paris for allies sports as competitor.	CW
	21.		do do 2/Lt. E.R. Giles from leave	CW
	22.		do do	CW
	23.		do do	CW
	24.		do do	CW
	25.		do do { 6 Capts. Commander visited the details of the Battalion. Capt. R.B. Burden & 5 OR to Damsti.	CW
	26.		do do { 2/Lt. B. Aulooth ww. to leave.	CW
	27.		do do { Major D. Benifels MC 2nd Lt. R. Re. as a/staff capt.	CW

WAR DIARY
or
INTELLIGENCE SUMMARY.

(Erase heading not required.)

Army Form C. 2118.

Place	Date	Hour	Summary of Events and Information	Remarks and references to Appendices
Beaufort	28.		Battalion supplying Guards relieving by in Emergency positions.	(Lt. E.R. Scott to course. 2/Lt. H.T. Allen leave. 2/Lt. C.E. Roe leave. 2/Lt. K.H.O.D. Hack France leave.
	29.		do do do do do do do	
	30.		do do do do do do Guards relieved by 2nd Northern Infy Brigade.	

Strength of Battalion 53/Off 940/OR
Nos. Present 23/Off 542/OR

[signature]
2/Lt. Adjt.
6 Bn. London Regt.

Headquarters,
2nd Light Brigade.
....

> Herewith 'War Diary' for this Battalion, compiled for the month of July.

31st July 1919.   ....Lt. Colonel.
                                   Commanding 6th Bn. London Regt.,

6th London Regt. Army Form C. 2118.

July 1919.

WAR DIARY
or
INTELLIGENCE SUMMARY.
(Erase heading not required.)

Instructions regarding War Diaries and Intelligence Summaries are contained in F. S. Regs., Part II. and the Staff Manual respectively. Title pages will be prepared in manuscript.

Place	Date	Hour	Summary of Events and Information	Remarks and references to Appendices
Elmsfeld	1.		Bn. moved to NETTESHEIM area in busses, arriving at mid-day.	(A)
Nettesheim	2.		General training & organization.	(A) At. A.H. Etaridge & Crowe. 2/Lt. G. macgregor to store service to 17th Bde.
do	3.		General Training & Education.	(A) 2/Lt. J.J. Bennett from course. Lt. Col. J.B. Brodey D.S.O. to leave. Major R. Patchett M.C. from Isle.
do	4.		General training & Education.	(A)
do	5.		do do	(A)
do	6.		Church Parade.	(A)
do	7.		General training & Education.	(A)

1577 Wt. W10791/1773 500,000 1/15 D. D. & L. A.D.S.S./Forms/C. 2118.

WAR DIARY
or
INTELLIGENCE SUMMARY.
(Erase heading not required.)

Army Form C. 2118.

Instructions regarding War Diaries and Intelligence Summaries are contained in F. S. Regs., Part II. and the Staff Manual respectively. Title pages will be prepared in manuscript.

Place	Date	Hour	Summary of Events and Information	Remarks and references to Appendices
Rutlesheim	8.		advance party proceeded to OHLIGS, to take over billets to from 5/6 Bn. Royal Scots.	M
Rutlesheim	9.		Bn. moved to OHLIGS by train. Took over from 5/6 Bn. Royal Scots. 4/OR to Paris for Victory march arriving at mid-day. Major J.A. Farrell DSO. from leave. 3/OR demobilised.	M
Ohligs	10.		2 Companies supplying guards & fatigues, remaining 2 companies carrying out training. Lt. L.H. Etheridge from leave.	M
	11.		do	M
	12.		do	M
	13.		Church Parade.	Capt. Rev. G.H. Beaumont C.F. from leave. M

WAR DIARY
or
INTELLIGENCE SUMMARY.
(Erase heading not required.)

Army Form C. 2118.

Place	Date	Hour	Summary of Events and Information	Remarks and references to Appendices
Allig	14		2 Companies supplying guards & fatigues, remaining two companies carrying on training.	CW
	15		do — Brig-Genl Rayn. came C.M.G. D.S.O. inspected the billets of the Bn.	CW
	16		do — Capt. C.E. Moss on leave. 2/Lt. J.T. Allen on leave.	CW
	17		do — 2/Lt. B. Lambert. rejoin from leave. 2/Lt. A.M. Russell on leave.	CW
	18		do — 2/Lt. X.H.O'D. Monde-Elliott from leave.	CW
	19		General holiday.	CW
	20		Church Parade.	CW

WAR DIARY
or
INTELLIGENCE SUMMARY.

(Erase heading not required.)

Army Form C. 2118.

Place	Date	Hour	Summary of Events and Information	Remarks and references to Appendices
Altof	21.		2 Companies supplying guards & fatigues, remaining one training.	(a)
	22.		Rhine Trip for Bn.	(a)
	23.		General Holiday.	(a)
	24.		2 Companies supply guards & fatigues, remaining 2 companies carrying on training.	(a)
	25.		do	Bn. sports for day, postponed owing to rain. 2/Lt. S. Macgregor from leave. 2/Lt. W. J. Lee " " Lt. Col. P.S. Brady DSO " "	(a)
	26.		do	Lt. G.R. Scott from canal. 2/Lt. X.H. O'D. Moule-ffinch hospital.	(a)

Army Form C. 2118.

WAR DIARY
or
INTELLIGENCE SUMMARY.
(Erase heading not required.)

Instructions regarding War Diaries and Intelligence Summaries are contained in F. S. Regs., Part II. and the Staff Manual respectively. Title pages will be prepared in manuscript.

Place	Date	Hour	Summary of Events and Information	Remarks and references to Appendices
Allipo	27		Church Parade.	CA
	28		2 Companies firing General Musketry Course & details. Remaining 2 companies carrying out training.	CA
	29		do	CA
	30		do	CM
	31		do Strength of Battalion 48/Off 877/OR numbers present 26/Off 569/OR	Capt. C.A. Fuller to leave Major B. Penfield M.C. to act London as 2nd in Command. 2/Lt. R.J. Cook to leave. 2/Lt. E. Morris to leave Lt. S.R. Scott from leave. CA

C.A. Fuller
Capt & Adjt.
6th London Regt.

WAR DIARY
or
INTELLIGENCE SUMMARY.

6th Bn. London Regt. Army Form C. 2118.

August 1919.

(Erase heading not required.)

Place	Date	Hour	Summary of Events and Information	Remarks and references to Appendices
Alligny	1		2 Companies find E.M.C. remaining completed training.	At L.A. Sgts. ratio (police) (A)
	2		Battalion sports in afternoon (heats &c).	At firms given to base (A)
	3		Church Parade	(A)
	4		General holiday. Battalion Sports (final) in afternoon.	(A)
	5		2 Companies finish S.M.C., remaining companies training.	(A)
	6			2/Lt. accompt. 17 men from Base (A)
	7			2/Lt Galbraith to base. (A)
	8			(A)
	9			Capt. Attershaw to Leave. (A)

WAR DIARY
or
INTELLIGENCE SUMMARY.
(Erase heading not required.)

Army Form C. 2118.

Place	Date	Hour	Summary of Events and Information	Remarks and references to Appendices
Alleys	10		Church Parade. Brig-Gen. Rum Currie DSO attended.	CW
	11		2 companies firing Spt. remaining companies training	CW
	12			CW
	13			2/Lt E.J. Millcock to leave	CW
	14			CW
	15		General Dudley. 2nd Lt. Bde sports	CW
	16		2 companies front Spt. remaining companies training	CW
	17		Church Parade	2/Lt W.J. Brown to leave	CW
	18		2 companies firing Spt. remaining companies training	Capt. C.A. Fuller from leave	CW

WAR DIARY
or
INTELLIGENCE SUMMARY.
(Erase heading not required.)

Army Form C. 2118.

Place	Date	Hour	Summary of Events and Information	Remarks and references to Appendices
Aldis	19		Battalion finishes I.T.C.	
	20		General training & Education	Lt. a.D. Ridden from hospital
				Lt. Col. E.B. Powell D.S.O. arrived
	21			Lt. Jno. Jordan from leave
				Capt. Rev. W.D. Iyffe proceeded on demobilization
				Lt. Col. J.B. Praig D.S.O. to
				Lt. Col. E.B. Powell DSO [?] Command of Bn.
	22			2/Lt. P.J. Eggar from hospital
				2/Lt. R.J. Reed from leave
	23		Church Parade	
	24		General training & Education	2/Lt. E. Morris from leave
				2/Lt. J.E. Sercombe to leave
				2/Lt. C.L. Cripps to leave
	25		do do do	
	26.			

WAR DIARY
or
INTELLIGENCE SUMMARY.
(Erase heading not required.)

Army Form C. 2118.

Instructions regarding War Diaries and Intelligence Summaries are contained in F. S. Regs., Part II. and the Staff Manual respectively. Title pages will be prepared in manuscript.

Place	Date	Hour	Summary of Events and Information	Remarks and references to Appendices
Abbey	27		General training & Education	Cal
	28			Capt Atteridge Jundiaia Capt F. C.A. Iwellers hospital Cal
	29			Cal
	30			2/Lt HB welcomes from leave Cal
	31		Church Parade	Capt CA Seller from hospital Cal
			Strength of Battalion — Off 4/ O.R. 804 numbers present 25 610	

A. Mills
Capt + a/Adjt.
6th Bedfordshire Regt.

WAR DIARY
or
INTELLIGENCE SUMMARY.
(Erase heading not required.)

6th Battn London Army Form C. 2118.
October 1919.

Place	Date	Hour	Summary of Events and Information	Remarks and references to Appendices
Oliqe	1.		General training and education	
	2.		Route March	
	3.		Platoon Drill and education. Capt. J.J. Roll from leave	
			Battalion Duties and Fatigues	
	4.		Billets and Kit Inspection	
			Baths	
	5.		Church Parade	
	6.		Inspection of Billets by Brigadier General Commanding 2nd Light Brigade	
			Battalion Duties and Fatigues	

WAR DIARY
or
INTELLIGENCE SUMMARY.
(Erase heading not required.)

Army Form C. 2118.

Place	Date	Hour	Summary of Events and Information	Remarks and references to Appendices
Ohage	7		General Training and Education Battalion Duties and Fatigue	OK
	8		Route March Battalion Duties and Fatigues	OK
	9th		1 Company – Platoon Training and Education 1 " – Baths and Disinfector	Major J.A.T. Purnell R.T.O. from leave. OK
	10		1 Company – Baths and Disinfector 1 " – Platoon Training and Education	2/Lt B. Lamberth rejoined from leave. OK 35. ORs to demobilization OK
	11		Billet and Kit Inspection	34. ORs to demobilization OK

WAR DIARY
or
INTELLIGENCE SUMMARY.
(Erase heading not required.)

Army Form C. 2118.

Place	Date	Hour	Summary of Events and Information	Remarks and references to Appendices
Allonne	12		Church Parade.	33 OR's to demobilization ⓦ
	13		Platoon Training and Education	ⓦ
	14.		Battalion concentrating into 1 Company on East side of Railway	25 OR's to demobilization ⓦ ⓦ
	15		Concentration of Battalion completed	Lt.Col. E.B. Powell D.S.O. to U.K. Capt. A.McLaine M.C. to leave. ⓦ
	16.		Platoon Training and Education Battalion Duties and Fatigues	2/Lt. E.D. Plimbu from leave 28 OR's to demobilization ⓦ
	17		Battalion Duties and Fatigues	8 OR's to demobilization ⓦ
	18		Battalion Duties and Fatigues	16 OR's to demobilization ⓦ

WAR DIARY
or
INTELLIGENCE SUMMARY.
(Erase heading not required.)

Army Form C. 2118.

Place	Date	Hour	Summary of Events and Information	Remarks and references to Appendices
Okupo	19		Battalion Duties and Fatigues	W
	20.		Battalion Duties and Fatigues	W.
	21.		Battalion Duties and Fatigues	
			2/Lt H.T. Allen from leave	W
			4 ORs to dem Obligation	W
	22		The following were posted to 13th Bn K.R.R.C.	
			5 Officers 85 OR with wind	
			2 " 5 " Detached	
			5 ORs to dem Obligation	W
			Total 12 Officers 142 ORs	
	23.		The following were posted to 18th Bn K.R.R.C.	
			7 Officers 96 ORs with wind Capt C.W. Bate to Army S.L.	
			3 " 28 " Detached 2/Lt B. Lambert " "	W
				2 ORs " "	W
			Total 10 Officers 124 ORs	

WAR DIARY
or
INTELLIGENCE SUMMARY.

Army Form C. 2118.

Place	Date	Hour	Summary of Events and Information	Remarks and references to Appendices
Chipe	23		Cadre of Battalion moved to new billets in MERSHEIS	MM

Smith Captain
Commanding 6th Bn London Regt.

www.ingramcontent.com/pod-product-compliance
Lightning Source LLC
Chambersburg PA
CBHW081500160426
43193CB00013B/2550